AF207112

For Lou –B.F.

For Andy and Olive, and for those dark
fishes with the spirit to look up and see . . .
–M.W.

Millbrook Press
A division of Lerner Publishing Group, Inc.
241 First Avenue North
Minneapolis, MN 55401 USA

For reading levels and more information, look up this title at www.lernerbooks.com.

Main body text hand-lettered by Michael Wertz.

Library of Congress Cataloging-in-Publication Data

Franco, Betsy.
    [Poems. Selections]
    A spectacular selection of sea critters : concrete poems / by Betsy Franco ;
Illustrated by Michael Wertz.
        pages cm. — (Millbrook Picture Books)
    ISBN 978-1-4677-2152-3 (lb : alk. paper) — ISBN 978-1-4677-8849-6 (eb pdf)
    1. Marine animals—Juvenile literature. I. Wertz, Michael, illustrator. II. Title.
PS3556.R3325A6 2015
811'.54—dc23   2014041354

Manufactured in the United States of America
1 – VI – 7/15/15

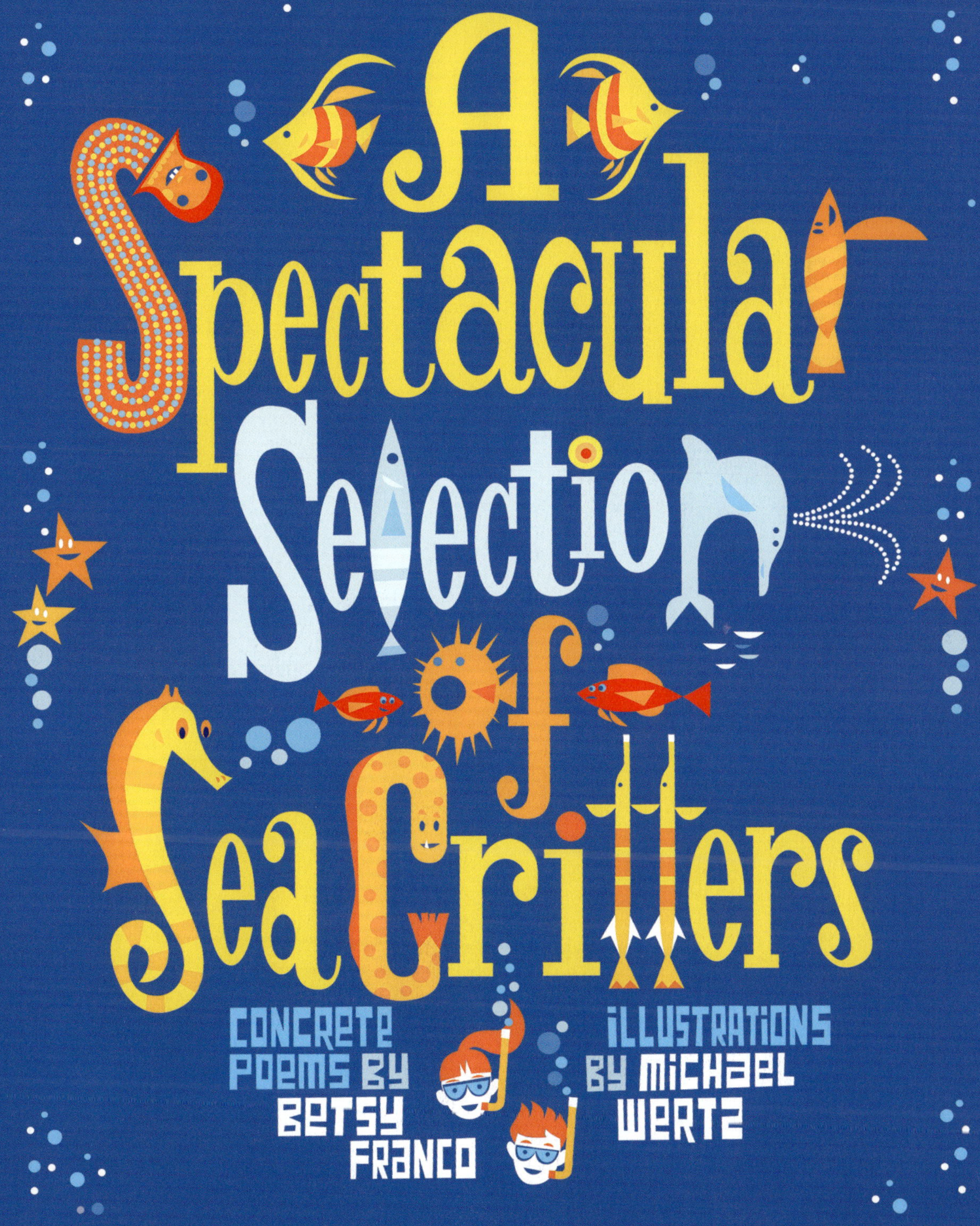

M MILLBROOK PRESS · MINNEAPOLIS

SUN MAIL
WARM WAVES OF SUNSHINE SEND OUT AN INVITATION:
SNORKELING TODAY!

Swimming in Schools

BOX JELLIES

YOUR ATTRACTION IS YOUR ACTION!
FASCINATING!
UNDULATING
PULSATING
NAVIGATING
...JUST DON'T STING ME!

Sea Turtles

You row by us
    with flippered "wings,"
you are such gorgeous,
    BULKY THINGS.
Since there were mighty dinosaurs,
you've laid your soft-shelled
    eggs on shores
where babies hatch
and dig out free
    to crawl back to

the waiting sea.

But now you're simply passing by.
Did you just look me in the eye?

NEEDLEFISH

NEEDLEFISH
NEEDLEFISH
LIGHT-LOVERS
SLIM
SLENDER
JUMPERS
SURFACE-SWIMMERS
TOOTHY
LONG-BEAKED

KING ANGELFISH

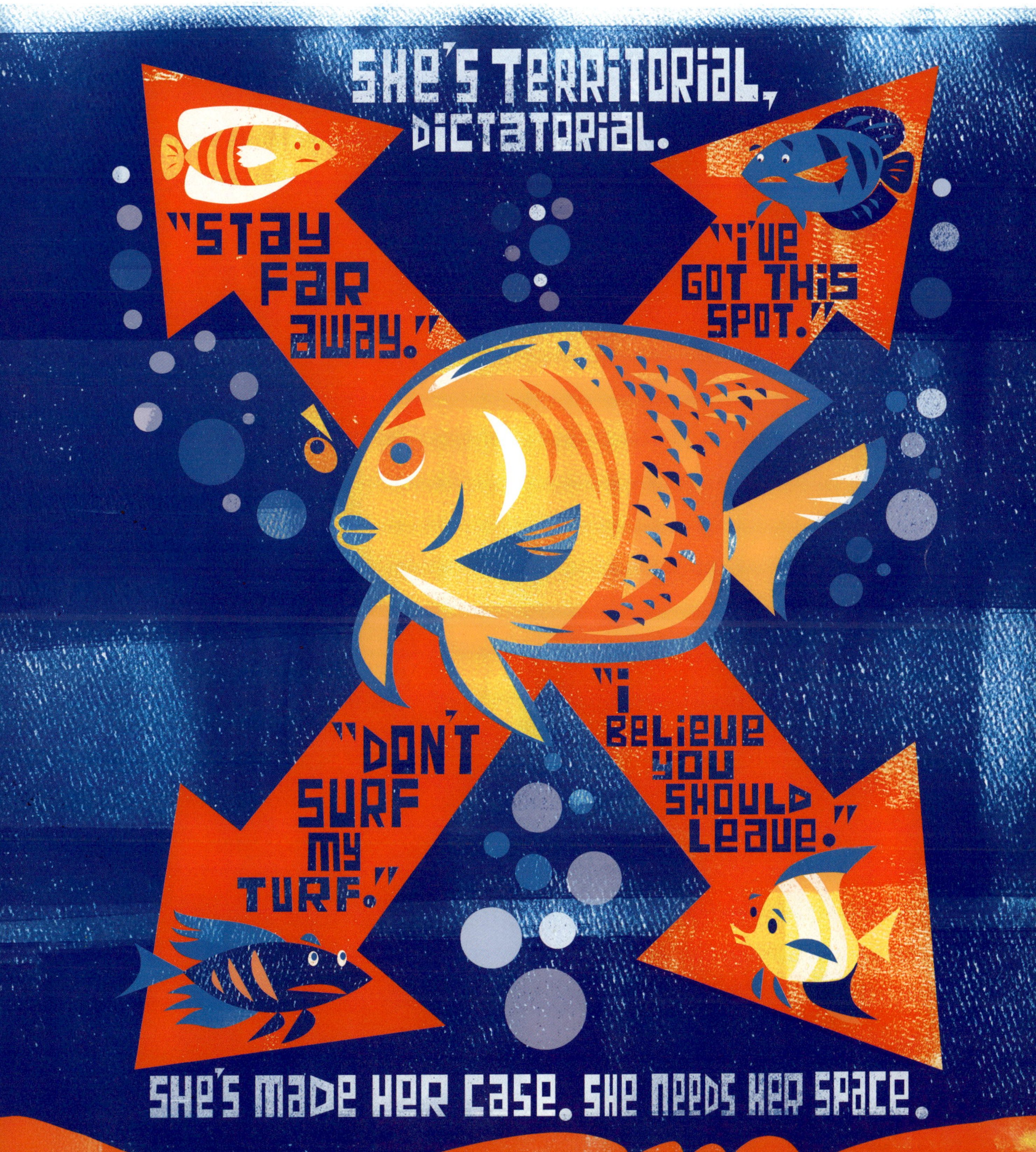

BUTTERFLY FISH
RIPPLING WAVES
BUTTERFLY FISH
CORAL
FLOATING,
FLITTING,
FLICKERING,
FLUCTUATING
FEEDING
FLEEING...
SILKY SAND SILKY SAND

WAVES
RIPPLING
THE EEL FROM THE
AND SO ARE WE!
SILKY SAND SILKY SAND

CLEANER FISH

SPINY PUFFER
YOU LIVE IN OCEANSCAPES.
BECAUSE YOU DON'T KNOW PORCUPINES,
YOU JUST MIGHT LIKE THEM
IF YOU DID,
'CAUSE THEY'VE GOT POINTY SPINES
WHEN PREDATORS COME CLOSE TO YOU 'CAUSE WE SMELL
A COMMOTION.
ALL MOTION.
AND STOP
BLOAT UP.
THE WATER IN.
YOU GULP
WATCH

FAIRY-TALE CREATURE, ANCIENT TRAVELER, TINY DRAGON, UNDERWATER QUESTION. WHAT TALES DO YOU HAVE TO TELL US?

BOLD
STRIPES
JAZZY COLORS
A HIGH SENSE OF FASHION
STYLISH & STYLISH
PUNCTUATED BY
TOP FIN!

THIS FISH LIKES TO HUNT FOR HER PREY
WHEN THE CORAL IS
NOT FAR AWAY.
SHE STICKS IN HER SNOUT
AND SUCKS A FISH OUT.
THE REEF IS HER FAVORITE CAFE.

FISHY NAMES

HAWK FISH.
LION FISH.
SQUIRREL FISH TOO.
FISHES' NAMES TELL WHO IS WHO.
CLOWN FISH.
PARROT FISH.
GOAT FISH TOO. FISHES' NAMES GIVE SNORKELERS CLUES.

RIDDLE POEM: WHICH FISH?

ANSWER: ME, THE SNORKELER!

STINGRAY

STINGRAY RESTING IN OCEAN SAND.
YOU'RE CAMOUFLAGED — BROWN ON TAN,
THEN, LIKE A GHOST, YOU RISE AND HOVER, A BILLOW OF BROWN RIPPLING AROUND. YOUR ARMS SPREAD WIDE, YOU GLIDE AND FLAP AND FLEE, THEN HIDE AGAIN AND DISAPPEAR. WERE YOU EVER REALLY HERE?

PARROT FISH
RAINBOW
CREATURES
GLEAMING
GLIDERS
CORAL
RANGERS
COLOR
CHANGERS
PUFFY
LIPPERS
PARROT
BEAKERS
ALGAE
MUNCHERS
CORAL
CRUNCHERS

Living upside down
Pretending to be algae
Waiting for dinner

THE
YELLOW
TANG
SOME
DAMSELFISH
ROAM
SWIM
NOT
NEAR
FAR
BY
DOES
MIGRATE
THEY
HOME
BLEND
IN
AND
OR
FROM
AND
LEAVE
IN
BLUE
INTERWEAVE

anemones

AT FIRST WE SEE A FLOWERBED
BUT THESE ARE ANIMALS INSTEAD.
THEY POISON PREY WITH TENTACLES.
THEIR MOUTHS ARE THEIR RECEPTACLES.

ACROSTIC: CORAL REEF

BOXFiSH / COWFiSH

REEF FOOD CHAIN

OCTOPUS

MOST OC-TO-PI ARE RA-THER SHY.
PLEASE, DO NOT TEASE. TAKE CARE, DON'T SCARE.
SHE'LL GET UP-SET, TURN RED, AND JET.
JET JET JET JET JET JET

AMONG
THE ANEMONES,
WHICH
POISON ALL
YOUR ENEMIES.
YOU'RE
SMILING AND
PLAYING AT
PEEKABOO
'CAUSE NOBODY
DARES TO
COME CLOSE
TO YOU.
YOU HIDE

UNDERWATER CASTLE

TERCET:FROGFISH
WITHOUT ANY SCALES, YOU LOOK LIKE A SLOB, LIKE CORAL OR STONE, OR A SHAPELESS BLOB.
BUT CAMOUFLAGING IS YOUR JOB!

SPINNER DOLPHINS
A POD OF DOLPHINS ROUND THE SUN, ARCING, SINKING, DIVING, DIVING IN THE SEA, ONE BY ONE.
SUN IS ALL WE SEE.
NOW CRESTING WAVES IS ALL WE SEE.
SUN IS SINKING.

SEA GLASS
SMOOTHED SPECIMEN WITH SURFACE SOFTENED BY SEA WAVES AND SAND SURFING

ASLEEP IN BED: DREAMING OF FISH

NEEDLEFISH
NEEDLEFISH
JELLY
TANG
BOXFISH
TRUMPETFISH
TRUMPETFISH
BOXFISH
TRUMPETFISH

FURTHER INFORMATION

BOOKS

Chin, Jason. *Coral Reefs*. New York: Roaring Brook, 2011.
Do you know what kinds of sea creatures live on a coral reef?
Or where reefs come from? Join a girl on an amazing journey
within the pages of this illustrated book and discover basic facts
about coral reefs.

DK. *Amazing Giant Sea Creatures*. New York: DK, 2014.
How big can sea creatures be? Check out the illustrations and
photos in this book to find out. From exploring where some of the
sea's biggest creatures come from to looking at what they eat,
this book is a good introduction to the world of the deep.

Fleisher, Paul. *Ocean Food Webs in Action*. Minneapolis: Lerner
Publications, 2014.
Explore the relationship between the meat eaters, plant eaters,
and decomposers of the ocean. Photographs and diagrams
help illustrate the relationships and connections among the
different sea creatures.

Owen, Ruth. *Marine Biologists*. New York: PowerKids, 2014.
If you've ever wondered what it's like to be a marine
biologist, this is the book for you. Find out how science
helps marine biologists do their job and what it takes to
study sea creatures in their natural habitat.

WEBSITES

Monterey Bay Aquarium—Live Web Cams
http://www.montereybayaquarium.org/animals-and-experiences/
live-web-cams
Take a look at live web cameras including the kelp forest cam,
Monterey Bay cam, and the Open Sea cam to see what kinds of sea
critters you can spot!

Shedd Aquarium—Animal Facts
http://www.sheddaquarium.org/Animals--Care/Animal-Facts/
Check out photos and learn about many different sea creatures
at this site created by the Shedd Aquarium in Chicago, Illinois.